Anonymous of Troy

Anonymous of Troy

The Early Books

Didier Coste

PUNCHER & WATTMANN

First published in 2014

Published by Puncher & Wattmann
PO Box 441
Glebe NSW 2037

http://www.puncherandwattmann.com

puncherandwattmann@bigpond.com

National Library of Australia
Cataloguing in Publication entry:

Coste, Didier
Anonymous of Troy: The Early Books

ISBN   9781922186683

I. Title

A821.3

Cover design by Matthew Holt

Printed by McPhersons Printing Group

This project has been assisted by the Australian Government through the Australia Council, its arts funding and advisory body.

Australian Government

Australia Council
for the Arts

When first they saw emerging from the sky,
That stranger bark in sullen silence sweep...

William Charles Wentworth

The voyage we do not take to the unknown
Becomes the poem that visits us instead ;

Alec Derwent Hope

Prologue

Figures on the Road near Abydos

How coy, how lascivious Helen really shone,
fretting alone in the fortress of beauty,
is of no concern to these coming stanzas.

Or how lenient to the frenzy of delight,
Hero from the stance of her squat tower,
scantily clad, by absolute will buttressed.

Reeling, endearing reeds of the valley road,
how lavish your gesture when we shiver
under a howling wind and dwindling stars!

***

Sitting on the porch in the dim reflection
of the work day, life amidst muted chores
calls local attention to some street lights.

I list those that failed long ago and those
that buzz and flicker with the inflections
of mosquitoes, a fickle, forgotten desire.

***

Peopled with figures of lions resting,
no more remains of a dream of pastures
but the acid backdrop of deciduous poplars.

Add a dash of red for poppies, dare a shade
of blue before the leaves veer to saffron,
let us wish colours that will not suffer.

***

We found a coin, nearly new and held it
with an ancient hand, so close to our eyes
we knocked once more on the baker's door.

The chance was he had sold the last loaf
but one; red chili was dangling nearby
and a flock of light clouds disbanding.

The foam of days no longer fools our sense
of being, a while, not aloof by the coast,
but deep in the muffled concert of things.

***

Maybe later on we can cycle to the crest,
we will order from the menu on the slate,
recover a taste for voice, acres of vista.

Suave water will trickle from the spring,
time is an entranced twig in the glass.
straight and stiff outward, twisted inside.

Time is but an illusion of its own class,
not our concern, not a threne of sirens,
it needs washing, with other edible roots.

The traffic of winds leaves it untouched,
time is the sister of the poem, the ring
and its stone, the bait of arrested twilight.

Part 1
A Dance And A Song

Still Dancing

Still dancing, dancing still, unending
list of songs, unsung but their lance
tilted to the heart, ever the very same,
its mace tearing at me, revered, both
sobbing and diverse, diving in lace,
tamely untimely, standing on the tar.

Soft in the distance, tough in its stance
the dance you set, you sent, and tense
when I saw your wonder, your woes,
winning once the red sun of your lips,
the lottery of your toll, this new simile
of miles, smiling on the lap of home.

Pale lime, fine slim lines of raw water
running still, nurturing the inner war
of feeling and leaves, in the late fall,
the winter really of Lear, while I read
your name, kite in the sky, that ticks
just here, to the cadence of the dance.

Out of the Blue

That there should appear out of the blue
a different girl, now without a pink fiddle,
but playing just for us and a select company
of virtual friends the single song of thin air,

that with her lyre, her sweet velvety voice
she should reap the ripe bulbs of our despair
and turn them into bright gardens of tulips
or fragrant dishes served outside in the spring,

that she can so easily shed our lines of verse
and for green the ginger hues of her hair,
and grant us the dashing flavour of her lips
and make terse again the creased days I bring,

that she should raid the nether world of gongs
with the sound of eligible silence, and camp
where the blockade of clouds opens to oblige
the whole vastness of my love and my disgrace,

that she should be voluble, and suddenly quiet
in the hushed rustle of leaves and sheet music,
this is not a dream, a bet, it is not smeared
by any simulation, doubt or Theban tragedy,

it comes in the perfect shape of kitsch angels,
in bar codes and the gilt coffee mugs of reality
with the rainbow digits of flying rugs and also
the broken English of your demanding body,

it displays the brandmark and quality labels
of our panting human lifespans in the city,
with the bravery of loving each other so,
with the animal presumption of staying hardy,

and, if it should vanish into the feeble notes
of remembrance, into the dire speed of the sea,
what would be left of the goodness of colours?
how brief and toneless our tunes would now be!

It is true such a blue girl parted the unseen,
her breath unfurling in the strands of a breeze,
without a guitar, her fingers braiding the air:
let the gods be pleased, let her breasts nestle here.

Near East

Is it you again, negated night, tiny Eastern sky,
verklärte feast, rosy point close to Eden and
crescendo, oddly appearing tag of the gods,
leading Babel on leash, signing the silky reign
of skin? Is it you my other, mother and kin
who clings to my sighs when, silent, I listen?

You it must be, now seeking the ultimate nest
of West, where to fall first in the arms of night
and fell its left, its lofty dice, its dark side;
with a long name whispered in your soft hair:
the tempered breeze of meaning floats around
your full face, nothing is safely the same again.

Ash, fun, fish, fable, unfashionable Lebanon:
behind we left the din of self-sufficient tales,
the tusks of thousand nights and one dream
of sands and a knight, and yes thou art coming,
dancing tight, hasty star from the mouth of East,
a sun at noon, my love, my will, meine Liebe.

Lark Ascending

Up and soaring, her rosy fingers a finch
tempting my empty hand with her wand,
this little fairy rises from the brittle shore
of a mountain lake, rushes in name, a noun
for the rounded azure, a proud colour for clay,
though it is about down here we speak, of hay
and sure fountains, a real dawn, a first blush
of bushes, the kiss of wheat and carnations,
but also the carnival of all the sick nations
with their crowded, unflinching capitals.

Early landed in Carthage, this age her part,
a world of limp luggage carts and souvenirs
gladly drowns and dwells near the prime rain
of joyful tears and swells and fills all its wells
and mimes the beauty of having a beer at the bar,
her ringed fingers the tinge of light, a set of stars,
her lower lip heaving high that my teeth plunder,
a bower and its hives through cigarette smoke:
soaring she thrives, the girl, bowing I regret
years of descent and I veer to her mirror.

Crawling trains of clouds over the sea
cannot hide the clarity of sense under them
where her unending flight resides and dances
within itself, its iris an ark and its scent a rose;
as the lark rose from the rents of one dark winter
she came into being and saw the spark of thunder
to wed flower and dew, to sew word with wharf
and join in joy the souls that were far asunder;
as she softly touched the hem of the goddess,
as the dancers above in light let her dress.

Nothing Ever Lasts

Nothing ever lasts for ever, save the veneer
of serenity, they say, on the wall of the law,
(when the law has been forcibly removed),
save white salt where the sea has withdrawn,
leaving logs, sirens and gulls who feed inland,
and twilight slow rising from a different pier.

But your science of me, this quiet acquiescence
to the twin vanity of future and past, this native
breast of knowledge that nurtures the last of us,
this is cast on the edge of wounded eternity,
it is made to outgrow the exhaustion of virgins
and the frowning storms of a maiden voyage.

Your own knowing, your feeling, beyond age
and distance, this is what forms the bastion
of imagination, as it prevails when we buy rouge
at the scent shop, and a bast to ride time
while it lasts, tense yet gouged from the urn
of earth, pushed back where it has no return.

The Tempest and You

There came a gale, all of wind and water,
its form dwindled, it faltered in the fall,
for nothing prospers that's not your make,
the tree was spared that we shall plant
and the tempered treble of the seashell
and the satiated taste of blackberry jelly.

The roof of our house was gaping broad,
the old oak was standing alone on the road
where no merry school bus would again stop,
look at me as I remain seated on the floor,
a happy fool no storm could hit at his post,
married and blessed, moored in the morrow.

Wild gusts blew our tiles, tore our shutters
from their hinges, the second light grew sour
on the fringe of nowhere and today's udders,
but we share fecund bulbs from this garden,
we'll mend the locks and the clocks of Eden
we can spare fodder for our seven flocks.

Such perfection a tempest brings in its wake,
we could forget to chase gasps and ghosts
and gibberish from the shapes of the real,
just as my dear daughter can catch the ape
pictured in every looking glass, or else
Alice's lust in the midst of streetfighters.

When cool oily lava, stale saliva and leaves
of grass spoiled the byways of our retreat
and soiled the chaste words of a young poet,
you alone saved us from their sticky flood,
the car slowly swerved before it stopped
at the top of the ocean, you were the wave.

Teased and Tossed

Teased and tossed from seat to debut dance,
desirous and besotted, such is the narrative
or epyllion from which the pure poem staggers,
its feet captive of movement, its daggers drawn,
its stiff pillars once more chained to change,
but flesh and stone are one temple for dawn.

Atonement, relics are not the order of the day,
ancient times are shelved, the present is plenty
and closed to traffic the porticos of nostalgia,
stalled the fickle corpse caught in seaweeds
and keeps your lamp, oh my ode, at the peak
of its sight, feeding on its own force, unfailed.

The poem not a scoop from Troy is the message,
the poem is the sage and his model together,
it holds its melody in its gaze, its game live,
unmoving but for eyelids in the thicket of horns,
its bold, new unicorn needs not be tethered
by joy or fear, it speaks the poem's language.

7/7

About every seven days, with their sheepish ream
of words, what was last spoken marks a pause,
sometimes I hate the seamless even ways
in which a sullen stream of truth flows
through those alleys of well-kept parks,
and I prefer, just for a while, the sullied,
the hectic pigeons that spark the fire of time,
the derelicts who kick themselves not their pets.

Alighting from the almighty streetcar of creation,
I can see you at my side, live little princess
of the present, with your shiny tin kettle,
sipping tea from a woman-shaped glass;
ripping heat from the heaped up colours,
you are, in flight, as fragile as the anecdote
but it is my reflection on the belly of the jug,
passing where you will stay, a mote in your light.

You say that peppered garlic isn't from your part
of the country, you dip your bread in some soft
creamy stuff, you tilt your head, you puff
your lips, I lick the tip of your fingers,
snug in the velvet of my fettered fate,
in the longer shadow of me cast by your lamp,
since it is the scene on which you set me free,
my endorsement and the letter of my credentials.

About every seven days, with their fiendish horde
of words, what was a token of the past flickers
in the fortunate dark of moon-grown glades
by your shy radiance (oh forward Lass)
open and spread under my treading feet,
for the future only blossoms on your face
and in the white-sanded alleys of your dance
—the maze of sound having finally found its chord.

Blind Bards

Homer, thought the erudite vultures of yore,
or maybe Ossian authored the famous lovers
who fuelled the ire of Aphrodite and Ocean,
they fathered also the entire famished lore
of singing sirens and mute monsters awaiting
solace, fathoms deep on the desolate rock bed.

This is because Abydos, Leander's proud abode
where I return, became another suburb of Troy
after Troy was burnt and Carthage destroyed,
all joy stifled, in carnage drowned, and erased
their native names from every bruised stone,
and baffled the heavenly bull by a cast arrow.

Home where you always were is reconquered
by carving in marble the most delicate conch,
the red cock hushed, the lion's mane tangled,
'tis my own task now to pull the searing dart
from the god's flank, and thanks will be given
for snakes unfangled and successful anglers.

Birth Shores

From your remote birthshores of Marmara,
as a dull Atlantic winter day was losing
here to the misty hinterland night of pines,
birches and sawmills the last of its ballast,
as the one note of the church bell summed
in its tight stroke the remnants of rumour,
you asked me in a murmur how I saw you
brinking to the forebank of my mind's screen:
then I shut my eyes to catch you breathing
fast in a thatched hut among date palms,
your strong ankles and rosy heels stealing
my own speed, healing the pernicious past
in the niche of your legs and your belly,
I could hear the robust waves beg and moan,
the jingle of harmonic bangles on your arms
and the wound of promise sealed for ever.

It was just you, I said, with no ornament,
the two of us playing tourists in our dream,
it was the low season, with a brisk breeze,
we lay in frayed jeans on the morning sand
between scattered footprints, bare and shod
and the matter of love, a single sunbeam
in your moist hair, tea with a touch of mint
on the unfurnished coast of the new year:
a land is soon forming, en route to the sea,
we can hardly guess its borderless contours
or forecast the force of the ideas that hoist
its lean trees and its steeples in the air,
we can only fend for its people, its restive
riches and that in the end they stay yours,
fond of their rest, untouched by endemic ennui
when novelty sails lone and I am no more.

Meteors

In the rain secretly singing the accretion
of grains to sand, of smells to signs, I melt,
I do not refrain from drawing lines of thaw
that mark a strange consent, to life perhaps
as a bird taps for the first time after the rain
and sounds a range of holes in the same tree.

After the rain clears and when our twin train
of thought has found a place to stop and post
in the oozing sap the dumb record of us two,
I take the past to the zoo, I lace it with tears,
I paste the pictures of bark huts and skin tents
on whose poles the poet counted native days.

Lost in the rain again, I grope and fumble
with the taste of your presence (umbrella,
hairpins, dedicated sunray), and the sense
—then— is no longer twisted in the fixtures
of roles, it is not cut or severed but borrowed
from the evidence of meteors and a home there.

Driving Thru

Slowly and distracted we shall drive through
whitish suburbs in search of a supermarket:
mightily attracted are the children by the shells
found on the permanent beach of balmy boredom,
and with you, my hands no longer on the wheel
as if there was a new target for daily wisdom.

What is it that wells up from the nothingness
of walls and railings and flat evergreen bushes?
what is it that swells and swings and rushes
without the smells of even an ailing spring
and makes us so glad that there we have been
clad in the attire of the mall's inner garden?

Slowly delighted we rove and float on the road
that leads to itself, the end where it started,
with cut flowers and vases on the next shelves
to the bustling exit where incense sticks burn:
we were ill so long with the rustle of things
but now that some meaning subtly rimes we heal.

Did you say you would buy the flowers yourself?
I see you are no longer afraid of sandglasses
or cry for the intensity of the sea in the city,
you can climb the imaginary dunes of reality,
immune to the street's advice you will rescue
for the sake of the wind a tall wounded horse.

Slowly and belated we glide under the billboard
that advertises a red convertible car in the sky,
one uninterrupted holiday at home and at work:
with travel, trip or folly our bloated eyes play
and our gullible minds for a brief moment mime
what we know is but a lost bluff, a trivial joy.

Yet this invisible loop we drew in the suburbs
also contains the dancing of your own language,
in which love is for the asking and each word
lilts and skips, and sends the birds that flew
faint but undisturbed over the pool of years,
dismantle at last the treasure trove of memory.

Achilles Was Here

Achilles was here and was killed on the siege
of this city where the quills of crows abund:
now the hills are dumb and deaf with the air
fed of stale pity and stiff morals, it is a tomb
that suddenly tumbled below the pale grey sun,
a blunt mound of clay under the canopy of peace.

Achilles, a stray cat licked your heel and cured
your furious pace, the feat made some peonies
blush, so long ago, in the pristine duplicity
of feral fever, betraying the plight of priests,
but the small heroic crowd there once was
has now vanished from the agora and the walls.

Achilles was here, his name was written on stone
entwined with the love of fame and the vines
of hurried glory, it is bitten by the lone wind:
an arrow was his viper and his sword a flurry
that ploughs its furrow in the mane of Thetis
as blurred lords of war carry away the piper.

So Transitory

So transitory is human life but love perpetual
transport and strife muted and abandon hampered,
on five fingers I count the towers of legend
that linger in your hands, the smallest flowers
of joy when red banners are raised by sunlight
over the port's many gulls fighting for fish:
back and forth in a sheaf of lagging feelings
we are born of this very ship to our oldest wish.

A delicate dove is evoked tiptoeing in the dust
of the open plaza, as if she brought to the mind
a younger swish of kissing in the urban grove:
the green and rosy thought itself, in the maze
of arrested time, takes the shape of the bird,
as if it could happen and fly among fishmongers,
or maybe it can, yes, if only we pause, dazzled
by the imminence of port, to light up and smile.

Unlanded we land and again unending, unfenced
we buy a cell phone to talk to the mother across
the hills, so close, sucking the milk of snow
to sleepwalk over the sea of that other loss,
we spill luggage (nuts, books, eau de toilette
and underwear) to gage the true depth of a gaze,
to extend the cubic net of a room, to let space
widen, a tune, a teen ode, some daring grace.

We order a small golden tea for you, the same
for me, the same always, please, for the bees
in its mirror, and Aristaeus waiting in the hall,
a patient man he is, taking bets in his fashion:
the shimmer of our discovery is fully explained
by the stars it sports, its softly indecent ride,
the pulse of powers pulled from our inner vanity
as a thick topping of honey for a weakling child.

You Want Me...

Being of the land, you trip on the liquid steps,
you state how brittle, how bloody is the sea,
you say a man is not meant to run and swim
but embrace the waist of a wife and her saddle:
walking barefoot never was an idea of the body
but of the spirit, all too frail to eat its prey.

You want me to wear boots, as I did many years
since, when I believed life was a funny horse.
Riding, then, was a matter of course, straddling
the back of each season, muscular and invisible,
but reason usurped the hooves of the young mare,
the morning pattern, divided, became a riddle.

Night has spread its bold print beyond the field
of desire, but we shall not let scripture's whim
hoard a faint future tied in its gordian bonds;
if the hounds of Hades howl in the fading light,
with felt we shall guard our heads from the grim
cold, and our tender heels with leather shield.

While Almonds Bloom

While almonds bloom anew, dry leaves race
and veer about the stable, such a small world
whirling among the stubble and a few remainders
of broken looms: something is thus revealed.

Something comes we had not cared to know yet
until it filled the crib of our common hope
and it was lifted to our lips and it quenched
the most ancient thirst and gave us repose.

Small makeshift houses along the river bed
scatter the vivid colours of narrow lives
at sunset: swift is our passage that arouses
teasing swallows in the dust of tattered stars.

It becomes all real, including the phone poles
on either side of the road, and one old man
astride his spattering two-wheeler, going home
and the moles on his daughter's round face.

We can see how the rubble of time heaps up
and autumn peaches will make savory sense
this year as they always did, we can enjoy them
for a fee, there is might in the prowling wind.

There is livelihood in the platter of mashed
potatoes and mixed salad we have on the bus
to Byzantium, the evening was ready to pat
a woman's loins and hum her bridal tunes.

Unheard of the brawling youth and the cloudy
herd that used to crawl across the empty sky,
our domestic fire crackles in the wild rain,
rhyming stanzas are shared, are whistled anew.

T'is getting dark over the flat roofs where
shadow stores the cradles of bygone days,
your limbs are in a mood to please the gods
and your own mouth with orange rind to play.

Quiet and stubborn, we fared for this moment,
we were born for it and reel with the sparks
that flared in the eyes of Eros and in those
of the fair robber of fire, not far from here.

Statues

Studs and knights by the written record reduced
to less than bone dust, may be honed in bronze,
or in marble honoured, their stories cheat us
of the chiselled poor, the superb wenches torn
and bruised in the suburbs, who begot their sons
and sold their teen daughters at public auction.

We saw lust wrenched from the stolen afternoon
by neat fighters, we lost our bearings, we seek
the higher branches of jasmine and oleander,
we covet the protection of the moon at midday
or those great lamps hanging from the rafters
of a dilapidated palace that was once our place.

But after uncountable centuries and a short life
of sorts, the statues of warriors and horses
who still camp in the open look lazily absent
from their glory and their virtues, they lord
only over the appraised decay of older oaks,
while we share the warmth of sentient animals.

A Sunset Poster

A sunset poster on the restaurant wall in Paris
on a par with the pervasive smells of roast
and chips, in the vague haze of an unloved city,
instantly rummages the sinful sense of calling
to the mind a bundle of other purple pictures,
but all kept at bay by the deciduous colours
of this moment when we are not yet embracing.

Is this what they call the inroads of modernity
that never rests or stops? the harsh spotlights
at the top of the hill chopping the nightly lanes
before dark? the sparks ground from tacit mills
to sharpen the merry-go-round of vain memories?
Is this what there is to cracking the glass pane
where lay for a while the fullness of the hour?

No banquet of divine meat, no blood libations
will ever be offered against the double slope
of Taurus, where that plastified nymph eloped
with the wine caskets of Bacchus and his grapes;
a shy, superfluous planet dived and sank behind
the tablelands of its own shame, but whoever
claimed I would join a rival team of attendants?

The single thin mystery that resists the reasons
of lithe reverie lies in the purest transparence
of photographs to the actuality of distance,
this is why we shall always prefer the uncouth
woods of the wild to the order of standard forest
and rest in the soothing violence of the wind,
not revel in the smoothness of facile thought.

Who loves you, you will wonder in those narrow
harassing streets? And what was revealed to him
by the whisper you can hear in damp inner rooms?
In slow circles pending answers curl about you,
hanging banners are suddenly blown by your will,
they can witness the queer manners of the people
who sleep in the dry tracks of their conquerors.

Rhythm

There is nothing so mysterious about rhythm,
it is what I somehow missed in younger years
because it crawled under the clout of anthems,
its bats didn't flutter, I missed it in a sister,
not even wolves howled or some snakes hissed
in the foul nightmares of my eternal winter.

Clumsy steps, awkward love, I relished fate
when I visited an old woman's deserted barn
and I lost the story line of her flimsy yarn;
famished hawks were evoked, woes cherished,
the afternoon went broke for the third time,
with fake birds I swooned as I would for sex.

At the passengers' exit, it became all different:
I did not wait, you had brought me with you,
a peer singer in the open space of your beat,
rhythm duly returned to the sky and the fields,
to loud children at play behind the mosque, to
the sea of drowned lovers, where clouds are few.

I Can Remember

I can remember so well our blue lagoon future,
the lewd bulbs of besmeared breasts in the dew,
the foam of days to come over many days gone,
their tiny babble, that infatuated contemplation
of time, and the milk drawn on a grassy farm,
the kiln in the yard, the ram in the paddock,
the drove of unwarranted hopes, the deep well,
its bucketfuls of fresh water to wash your face,
our wishes granted, the truth of baked bread,
I can remember every sip of the raspy gold wine
poured to pouting lips from green glass jars.

We can guess the soggy weight of laundry, shirts
and skirts lifted to the clothesline, wet pins
in the frost, the soft texture of sifted flour,
garage sales, sundries, when new skies move in:
Aphrodite rages in the lace of elegant oblivion,
let her soak in the sea of origin, let her weep,
a house is now being furnished in this world,
with olives for breakfast, a legacy of dreams,
a bannister of brown varnished wood to climb
to the sassy conversation of our bed upstairs,
finally clad in the garb of our actual desire.

Round shoulders and silky skin, our kisses shall
sound in the folds of your flesh, in the shell
of an ordinary spring, far from the ford of myth
and the filth of swords in deafening battles:
definitely free from the drab shackles of whim,
we returned all the diamonds of ancestral lore.
As we go uphill under a hardened arch of blue
toward a rocky crown of mounds and boulders,
we march on the road where a haughty gardener
sells small trees to grow in the school grounds,
we pass a three-legged horse, we smile on him.

Still Singing

Still singing, subtly settled, singing still,
The bountiful bust of my bouncing lass,
The chosen choir in your single voice
Risen from the lavish valleys of earth,
Still courting the unique nudity of night
And the passing mirth on its mountains.

With sore fingers, gold rings and the jingle
Of cattle bells in the battle of the wind,
They pluck roses from their ample skirts
That dwindle in the folds of the dells,
Still growing plump fancy fruit in rows,
Still dancing to the drum and the flute.

Bright eyes, sky blue, sea green tidal lull,
How slow are the fires, how fast the hands
Of the last song: you admire its embers,
You smear its ashes on your bright brow,
Now you are the song, not its mere sound,
Singing still, the waking, not the slumber.

Part 2
The Crossing

Çanakkale

1

Regal once was the water edge and hoarse the voice of its herald
come from older frost, sprung to this ring.

As the seasons fold to a close, the near seclusion of the sea locks
and ruffles on themselves almost its quills.

My mind and my will, both dwell by a quiet harbour on the straits
though resounding with the labour of sirens.

A warring love of the land's paling on the flanks of voluntary hills,
I shall not lend more hands to memory's mosaic

Or exchange these sparse archaic words for the bright green sign
of beer dispersed in front of a model mosque.

Clouds will begin their night shift pouring a wide range of purple
proud yet equal to most bygone expectations.

Divinity lies in its own vines, revolves about invisible hinges
and for the usual city lights again we cheer.

2

Irreversible once were those waves that spoke in sibling tongues
gaunt, gull-poked, in irregular shades woven.

Facing the coast, a world of stable colours comes sit at our table,
we want to bear a toast to time as it passes.

While the domes of heaven are slowly dissolved for breeze's sake
seaside cafés take in wafts of new knowledge,

The same moods and modes of the water edge they share with you:
you'll decide whether these feelings are fake.

And I leafing through the same shifting maze of soft—bellied kites,
would eye the tan of Eastern winds at sunset.

Young men and girls wrapped in the cloth of air vow the moment
to the neatness of eternity, now their host.

This is when we both know we found a reason to be in this perfect
place, with one lamp post blinking the beat.

3

The straits show another gallery where once the bellows of Aeolus
hollered, but their harshness now smothered.

The stillness of the mall, a starched flow of stars is not restrained
by the restless oily foam in the ferry's wake,

Flutes and cherries are lifted and blown to full flavour by Sezen
Aksu's song, snowing flakes of terse petals,

The tepid riches of an empire, when lost, take the accent of truth,
all underwater rocks are of one make at core.

Hours circle the pier, complete their easy dozen and then we shiver
when this late spring begs its early winter.

The old bazaar is about to shut, our sleepy souvenirs entrusted
to the hazards of an evening, looting, rust,

Our voices, similarly hushed, no longer hoist netloads of fish
but float small, long-winged emotions instead.

4

Equal once was this water front to the myths and delusions of Egean
adventures beyond, poisoned flammable horses,

Rumpus, havoc, coarse sacrifices, but indentured Sisyphus is prompt
to cancel mortgage on his Barbaros apartment,

In retirement we might share with him a clean grey marble landing
and garbled echoes of some teenage TV series.

All the forces of praise and blame are now poised in due balance:
of the giant merry-go-round one beast remains,

So tame that nothing could lurk behind the raised flags of feast,
or only a few moonrays for the sense of place.

If you test the tense colour of peace, the breadth of this haven,
pray do not forget you built it so far inland

That the mature sting of olives or walnuts on our plates is gleaned
from the hill slopes, the oval glades of ever.

5

Of virgin Gaia born Pontus once was the road by all sails trodden
and stormy-stepped was his incestuous progeny.

The margin of belief lay at the door of Sestos, an elongated edge,
a tight leafy feeling, away from ochre steppes.

This is why we live no longer on the scale of lexical continents
but on the kofta and fruit of an orderly shore.

Surprise and wonder arise from the accuracy of the digital camera,
as your own palm shoots us free and unframed:

In the care of two, a hotel row, sifted pollens and the unmitigated
pledge of gazing yonder in each other's eyes.

Half drawn the curtains of both lands, there is no end to sunset,
hymen, alexandrine rings, there is no curfew,

We'll cross back to Eceabat, grant ourselves this soothing reward,
the froth of dawn, the body in its fairest light.

The Reef of Dawn

Now that all these skinny chairs idly sit on the untidy sidewalk,
now the wretched fall of footmen is apparent

But it's too late for their parents to mourn the defeat of the day,
the opal sheen of milk has long been skimmed

And stripped of iridescence, there barely remains in the distance
a glow of fled helmets over some matted hair,

Blood at the helm, the forlorn instance of courage running slow
toward its destiny, its abstruse, maimed crags.

The hooves of the royal horse are now hanging in the chilly air,
we can only hear its loud screeching wheels,

The pain of such a remote past, the dregs of forgotten beverages
now cast into the baleful furrows of war songs:

Of sturdy wood were made the wheels, of bronze the equine soles
and again they break against the reef of dawn.

The Rest of the Stroll

Lightly etched, our eyes touch the waning imprint of vacant chairs,
not all of them proceed from the same dream,

Some evoke teatime and some, made of tubes and imitation wicker,
can repeat the most banal patterns of feeling.

The fruit stalls, spilling out on the road, show no sense of limits
or strictures, Apollo is painted on the uneven

Walls of the heavenly cave, his liquor fills the canal of nations
while oval seeds stick to our buskins mildly;

This picture echoes the cavalier heart riding in alternate steps
the gigantic forest and a wench's thin skirts.

The hem still flimsy, the mauve skin under it tightens to the cold,
it shivers exposed to Troy's antique flames:

Your joyful world has invested my mind, the sore spirit surrenders
to the sketch of swell, the rest of the stroll.

Wishes Granted

Awash with the wave, the shawl of the sea, as if the law of wishes
had ashes deleted, turned to matter of reality,

Rusted the war-axe and flawed the seals of wax in a dreamer's ears,
all the shields are smashed and the oars mossy.

Peace has come where sword and words are safely stacked in the sash
of bulky cowherds, laden with cheese or fruit:

They weekly ride the minibus down to town, for post and hospital,
they sip hot bronze from tulip-shaped glasses,

A new ladder leans to the wall, the present will not be postponed,
its song furled in the folds of perennial lips.

Like them I too strove for the heaving flowery haunches of wives,
I fawned over female demeanour, weaving baskets

of fluid rush, and the fastest crest of the sea I climbed once only
to find beauty's face lies this side of the sun.

Knowledge Reconsidered

1

Why the shore, the edge, where there is no rift, rather a bridge
between the stiffness of yore and the supple

Ridge of today, where the ruminant raised land has deftly braided
its winding roads and so doubled our strength?

Not the window, not the view, but the very breathing of being here,
ships on due course, ordinary families, lovers

Endowed with steady wind, the ever moving orb of constant thought,
they all mill around a ray of sun, a golden hue.

The immensity contained within the opposite coastline and this one
is so homely under the fresh limelight of dusk

That your city reflecting its pastel site across the blueish flood
could play host to the plundered bays of mine.

We shall sit for a while on a bench of the English garden and hear
its sparrows attuned to the coming chime of rain.

2

I really wonder why prosperous men build their many-gabled villas
a good half mile from the shiny marine expanse,

As if by brutish Poseidon relayed, wrapped in his rumbling thunder,
a dead father bragged he would return unharmed

And by drums announced in the leathery garb of a stinking monster
sink our boats, warp our faith, gobble our youth.

But this could not happen now, with myth and reality split asunder
and such quiet spread over the measurable bodies

Of land, sky and sea where protected peacocks and impish girls vie
for lean crackers, pearls and zirkon glimpses.

Orderly teams of idle clouds watch over the sleep of Idomeneus,
the Trojan princess is busy with needle work,

No distress will reach here, I really wonder why we should not mock
the loud barking, the crows, and the eclipse.

3

Oh my tiny one, let us not open our yard gates to a defunct storm,
pleasure and reason have hatched in coral hands,

Unmarred the sungod has pinned a high note on his definite horn,
the season chose to become light and profound,

The larder and cellar are stocked with tasty game and fine wines,
we can see fellows of the phenix hastily flock

To sing and praise anew, the same long forgotten ode I once knew,
the song that lay warm in the baker's cradle.

Guests were warned to leave their muddy shoes on the festive mat
where our purring cat hails, meaning no harm,

We are well read and taller, as charm prevails we trim our hedges,
we tidy our thoughts in horror of scaly hubris,

The distorting mirror we fought shows no smudge of the irate gaze,
it is now as clean and tacit as the sea can be.

4

The stones were young in a young world with which they built a fort
and too short-lived the uplifting of standards

For you and me not to see how fragile was the pride by Priam flung,
as high only as his splendid dagger could fly.

Rough-hewn blocks have aged so fast in an era of subtler rhythms
or more futile, the inane wilderness of flowers

Is locked in bottled perfumes that clog the bathroom glass shelves
and, not Zephyr, sighs even wider in my rimes.

Puzzled dusty faces, the paired halves of symbol almost meet across
the two-way flux, the fir-lined banks of time:

You combed your hair at its open window, you brush aside the mass
of alien memory with your swift married hand

And we gladly realize that the mood of this moment belongs to none
of the many lost tragedies of Homer the New.

5

Beauty today is as it was, singular and immaterial but supported
by shape, light and volume as they now appear

Gaping fearless in the third dimension of wide angular photographs,
overtly assumed by the hoorray of serial muses.

It is therefore difficult to imagine the bold stench of surrender,
the brutal cult of dead flesh in the ditches,

How rarely the gender of Troy joined the folds of the sea to bathe
grave itchy loins, or hear their loud joy then.

Sky effendi is no longer smeared by those hazy clouds of history,
when offal was pledged to pacify the dark gods,

Skewers are merely barbecued for a country breakfast on Saturday,
the dogs of destiny bark farther from the pass.

This is why, my tiny one, we crave for mere fudge, some new sense
by childish mouths issued, not their fathers.

Preserved Buds

Sense, I mean, new to us or restored in full view of the living,
as when the vines of Spring invade the stairs

To suggest a shy shivering nymph, or the unexpected fuss of snow
has just melted and another unicorn is weened.

Hence a bewildered guide would show in jest the tarnished silver
of dry rosebuds among the bones of the newborn,

But today having hired a small red car to climb up to hefty views,
the loose belt of the Milky Way comes undone.

You have thus unlaced your mind, presented yourself with this gift:
the crisp-sounding privacy of your own stage,

Its gates flung open, clear of skulls, spectres, ivy, not sulking,
fed with fresh figs, tolerant with the seeds

Of mulberries in the lot of yesteryear, and even the stubborn wasps
lisping, slipping out for a meal in the fields.

Troy, the Film

Among those poor treasures dug out from the dung of later cavalry
and now fast eroded by acid rains in the open,

A tale of past slackness is moored, scanty feathers of a stray hen
and the unsaid, unfinished task of rival cocks.

When this story was penned on rock, when one could feel the pain
in one's own doomed heel and relish godly rape,

I thought I had a home, a golden casket sealed in its foundations,
my return, half a lifetime, to the dog of glory.

The odes of today, reflecting his face in the chromes of modernity,
have set a velocious mood for the elated hero;

The engine under the hood, instant mail affinities make a mockery
of trivial data, concerns for food and progeny:

Though not bent on nostalgia, we cannot pitch our fragile tent apart
from where the burnt horse rests after the show.

Remembering the Heroes

The first and the last fires happened here, when half-naked hordes
of stiff warriors just out of their thirsty nap

Broke open with their fists all the foul doors of Hell's kennels:
so many felled the leafy barriers of decency.

Rabid at core, that descent of Titans knew passion but no feeling,
when from the primal wave their tainted gaze

Beheld the curly rise of Aphrodite, brown hennaed designs, erudite
tritons, or one Helen under the horizon recede.

Grumbling, burly, ranting, those short men of unlikely flesh tinge
and unreason prodded goats as in vintage porn,

Unlike us they dashed for a tin crown and deplored the finer arts,
their minions sold stale bread to the besieged.

Trembling and rhymeless, the heart is our prison, and thorny eyes
flash the prodigy of hearing disembodied voices.

Land of Virtue

1

Should you ask me, I shall not pine in the least for the dwellers
of the inaccessible lair there was, the Eastern

Land of fancy well-doers where we now enhance our typical regret
for balloon sleeves and black silky stockings.

Oh, before departing for the ancestral valley of shadows, they held
the slack tree of genesis in their loony fist,

They called it a sceptre, they clashed with other kings and widows,
their sisters took revenge on setting cesars.

But on site in our shared reverie, things look a lot less sinister,
rather like a cool decor for a driving school,

Look here, the rocks are bare, clustered stars have stopped moving
a long while, you can almost hear them whining

For the last time, you can bend with me across the twenty-four sills
of the abyss, its own magic of missing flowers.

2

When the tempered chord was struck, when the cool weather arrived,
when pheasants were revered for their colours,

When the emotion of a future began fluttering, and we, all flustered
humans took time to build mirrors, polish verse,

Then the folly of having been —other than we are— became apparent
even to the less gifted gods and mere survivors

Of the flood: aloof in the rain, sifting pollens, cursing mothers,
we decided to live, we shrouded the arid hills.

As blue beehives were planted between the broken columns of Assos,
or tall wind mills to deride the solemn clouds,

A wiser Aristaeus would disperse wingless souls, clean acrid mires,
confine naked snakes to their fearsome caves,

Never again will he pursue his perfect sister on her wedding night:
please brink free, bride of the honeyed lyre!

3

Free from hackneyed metaphors, born where eternal trees take over
but breathing within range of this tidal time,

As free as a drop of dew in the web of morning desire, you strain
the tenacity of myth, rob it of its prestige.

We can also sit outdoor, for the actual voice of the owl and frogs,
a cooler embrace, a bowl of milk on the fringe

Of the simple past, not fooled by the grace of dryads, not ravished
by their delicate pace on the kilims of empire.

Free from prejudice, our limbs duly ointed against mosquito bites,
we have drawn two garden chairs to the porch,

Not far lies the sea from its reflection in your eyes, the orchards
of what there is, its fairness, its patience:

New songs are glowing on the lawn, music is a warden of the mind
whose lavish pyre slowly crumbles into night.

4

Yes, I know, capricious long-eared animals will not toil and play
or be pronged to their knees in moonless land,

The feared flow, the throng of time is flailed by the sooner masses
of world weather forecasts, droughts and floods,

So that the new roads do not softly curve with the kneaded folds
of cows, primeval pastures and hand-sown crops:

We plead to the vain wind, to the eves of old houses, to the awnings
where tools rest and thought turns into dream.

We read between the white lines of invisible planes in their sky,
not ours, the few hours that will be our lives,

The claims of flagged nations, the fast fullness of being in flight
where nothing happens but brute metal, reality

At its highest —hovering over our local ploughed plots, the tags
of familiar faces, vocal quietness at long last.

5

Between a whiff of jasmine and a streak of blood on the girl's leg,
ancient travellers would twirl their idle tracks,

Oh, wanderers, how you revelled in the spasm of cracked memories,
how you sat on the ledge of the mountain, crying,

But the wilderness within, filling the mouth of Scamander, I want
to crown all along with the scandal of flowers

Milling from the pigeon-blue edge of harbour to the bowers of Ida,
to the tall cliffs where hanging creepers grow.

Mending the embankment a deeper hush covers the sound, a subdued
blush dawns over the mound of singular presence,

In the sandy distance the last carts clanking remind us of the dew
to come, the home that will not be destroyed:

For the fitness of the day I shall clench and open this right fist
and witness the mighty fall of scented petals.

Epilogue
Four Idylls

Idyll 1

A place by this name *brook*, this name *field*, would be
with supple furry, with winged neighbours,
none of them bored, no lisp of the poem,
with many flowers, and the manes of opulent clouds,
by this name *dere*, this name *alan*, together
in agile weather, ready gold, never guilty,
it would be weightless, untied from the loops of time,
with twilight pools, lanes dear to my heart,
with its clover smooth and polished bowers,
a place it would be to live at length in this world.

Where the bluish shore licks fences, where jetsam
will never be needed, where the ballast
of nostalgia lasts not longer than the day,
this is where rushes with a double moon are brushing
sofltly, this is where the veteran peacock
has fallen silent in front of its rainbow,
where a single ball of straw seems to be its own sun,
picking a pace of leisure, all but killed
by the first rusty leaf that flies at noon,
this is where the tassels of time hang from its beak.

A place by this name *dere*, this name *alan*, would be
with ruffled purple, with rosy-tinged doves,
safe from the salt of death in boxes kept,
safe from all the sleazy things that dive in the dark
of the world's mind, doomed by the lack
of a name one would call *brook*, and *spring*
—unlike this enchanted place where time was spliced
by the four hooves of your running horses,
equal day of Apollo in slight variations
over a place where at long last lightly we could live.

Idyll 2

With fields on either side free-flowing down the slope
where the house nestles in the morning light
till the last dice of sundown are thrown,
with the tail of a passing comet still on the horizon,
a teasing sour yellow of fresh flower beds
and a folded list of our smiles in my hand,
we can see how hard the present wrestles with the past
and steadily rises to the entirety of time,
we can see how a mild spring sires distance,
we can feel every leaf, the ringing of every chime.

Feeding on milk, honey, in defence of sweet kinship,
morning and vesper stars are lamb-clad twins
slow-twinkling at opposite ends of a swing,
skimmed of blame's froth, cleansed of rats and silos,
they outline the site of all possible wings,
they cut the cloth that will keep us warm,
they face each other across the peak of only love
while our fragrant pantry harbours safely
in earthen jars the stuff of our fulfilment,
and herbs in the garden feast to enliven our meals.

Sentry oaks have healed the wounds of man's old wars,
we can hear through the wooden door ajar
the hushed dialogue of cool and sultry air,
or, in the winter, the names of coal fire and icicles,
we no longer watch, we touch the sandglass
and turn this twined bliss, this open ellipse
of sleepy hours, we turn it upside down once again
before the fast wheel comes to a standstill
before the cat drowses on the window sill
and the circular moon drowns among the valley reeds.

Idyll 3

Time has come and gone, it is coming, glow and gleam,
embers and stream at once, flames return
every week when we stack the open air oven
beyond the shed, in a place by name *spring* and *hill*,
in this place by name *pınar*, by name *tepe*,
when we stack with dry lumber the clay womb
of nourishment, the vow of plenitude cast in a dream,
and then run in slow motion toward the bench
and sit and partake of the claims of air
with the sheer might of time, its mills in the plain.

The clear chambers of night are equal to those of day,
tiny sunrays veer to the side of rosy limbs,
a boy that is not me skates down the hill
and clambers back up to where fresher delight awaits
his thirst with a notion of eyes as lakes;
the baked heart of our bread remains tender
when torn by chubby hands: "oh mother, see the thorn
in my palm, the bush bleeds, not my flesh,
I found the squandered fruit to feed on,
all dread was quelled, my life doesn't hurt any more!"

Liquid seasons have twirled about the roots of time,
they can dispense with memory, for the dead
too smile unscathed, free of mystery tours,
they thwart the stalwart reminders of armored minds:
here the doorbell rings the rimes of robins
in this tall place by name *hill* and *spring*,
where green spruces grow beside our leisurely meals,
in this place by name *tepe*, by name *pınar*
where the boundless stanza framed in air
will bring to completion the rounded promise of scent.

Idyll 4

You passed unknowing the audible threshold of harmony
as you would rock into effortless sunrise,
you have reached the mellow core of the wood
where no harm can come to you, where all the tempting
berries, red, or black or blue, are edible
in this place by name *new*, by name *village*,
you recognise every twig, all the many hues of sage
in this fresh place by name *yeni* and *köy*
where a star twitched nightly and few are
the barriers between your body and the river below.

Mild and strong is the honey bees bring to this land,
its denizens it lulls into never-ending joy,
of one will they coil on their wide beds,
they divide the vast throng of wanderers and cross
the trough between the breasts of eternity;
where Leander to his bride last returned
is no rocky cliff but the blessing of plentiful crop,
our stone and timber home rests as light
on the land as a tent would of white cloth:
you ride the visible, you are the warden of willows.

When it is time to air the quilt on the window ledge,
when the doves' lilt gathers in the breeze
the slow tea and olive hours before midday,
a wonder child is fathered on the winding road yonder
to move through the golden span of the poem;
no one, not even the dean of widows needs
remember how long the grove, the child have been new,
this is what makes it easy to live broadly
in a lost garden, culling plums and quinces
wild as they will issue from the tree of the present.

www.ingramcontent.com/pod-product-compliance
Lightning Source LLC
Chambersburg PA
CBHW031006090426
42737CB00008B/707